I0823125

THE SEARCH FOR BIGFOOT

Kevin Cunningham

Mitchell Lane
PUBLISHERS

Mitchell Lane
PUBLISHERS

mitchelllanepub.com

2001 SW 31st Avenue
Hallandale, FL 33009

First Edition, 2026.
Author: Kevin Cunningham
Designer: Ed Morgan
Editor: Morgan Brody

Series: Into the Unknown
Title: The Search for Bigfoot

Library bound ISBN: 979-8-89260-739-1
eBook ISBN: 979-8-89260-740-7

Photo credits: cover, 2, 4, 32 freepik.com; p. 3, 4, 15, 23 Shutterstock; p. 5, 7, 9, 11 wikimedia; p. 13, 17, 19, 21, 25, 24, 27 Alamy

CONTENTS

CHAPTER ONE

BLUFF CREEK

It happened on October 20, 1967. Roger Patterson shot one of the world's most famous films.

Patterson visited Bluff Creek in northeast California. He took a movie camera. Patterson believed a giant creature lived in the nearby forest. Other people claimed they had found its footprints.

His friend Bob Gimlin agreed to go along. The pair rode horses. At the creek bed the animals became nervous.

Gimlin spoke to KNKX.org years later. "There was a Bigfoot standing there just on the other side of the creek from us," he said. "But it just immediately turned and started walking away."

CHAPTER ONE

Patterson jumped off his horse. He ran and filmed. The camera shook. Patterson stopped. He steadied himself.

The female creature stomped toward the woods. It looked back at the men for a second.

The pair followed on horseback. But the mysterious **cryptid** disappeared.

"I didn't have time to be scared," Gimlin told CBC.com years later.

The 59.5-second movie became known as the Patterson-Gimlin film. What the camera shot didn't impress Gimlin. But Patterson earned money showing the footage.

The Patterson-Gimlin film made Bigfoot famous. People everywhere recognize the image of the creature looking back. Bigfoot became an **icon** in the Pacific Northwest. Shoppers can buy items like Bigfoot dolls and holiday ornaments.

But the stories about a hairy creature had started years earlier.

A Bigfoot museum in Willow Creek, California

FAST FACT

Bigfoot believers gave the name Patty to the creature in the Patterson-Gimlin film. Patty is named after Roger Patterson.

CHAPTER TWO

SOMETHING IN THE WOODS

At least 18 First Nations belong to a group called the Kwakwaka'wakw. These **indigenous** peoples live in British Columbia, Canada.

John W. Burns taught school. He lived near the Sts'ailes (sta-hay-list) in the 1920s. The Sts'ailes are a Kwakwaka'wakw nation.

Sts'ailes people told stories and sang songs about sasq'ets. These wild people lived in the mountains. Sasq'ets protected the land and the Sts'ailes.

CHAPTER TWO

Burns wrote down details. He reported sasq'ets as giant humans. They wore their hair long. Burns turned *sasq'ets* into the English word *Sasquatch*.

In 1957, a nearby town promised a $5,000 reward for a live Sasquatch. The town hoped to attract visitors.

It worked. Sasquatch hunters arrived. The stunt attracted worldwide attention.

William Roe reported a sighting soon afterward. Roe spotted a female cryptid while hiking.

"It was covered from head to foot with dark brown silver-tipped hair," he wrote. Roe also described wide feet.

FAST FACT

The town of Harrison Hot Springs invented the 1957 Sasquatch hunt. The Harrison Sasquatch Museum opened there in 2024. The Sts'ailes share their culture at the town's Sasquatch Days every summer.

CHAPTER TWO

Roe's creature sounded nothing like the sasq'ets. But his description stuck. Future sightings usually mentioned a hairy, **bipedal** creature.

Ray Wallace built roads into the woods. In 1958, he found giant footprints near Bluff Creek, California.

A worker poured a material called plaster into a print. The plaster hardened. The worker showed people the plaster "footprint."

Workers for a California newspaper named the unseen creature Bigfoot. Later, Roger Patterson went to Bluff Creek because of Wallace's prints.

Bigfoot sightings took off. Soon people spotted the cryptid all over the United States.

FAST FACT

The largest Bigfoot prints measured 18 inches (45.7 centimeters) long and 8 in (20.3 cm) wide.

CHAPTER THREE

BIGFOOT COAST TO COAST

Believers in Bigfoot call themselves Bigfooters. People all over the world belong to the Bigfooter community.

Certain Bigfoot stories stand out. Bigfooters say the sightings provide **evidence** of the creature.

Bigfoot sightings occur often in Western Pennsylvania. In 2007, hunter Rick Jacobs placed a camera in the forest. He hoped to photograph deer. The camera snapped a hairy bipedal creature.

CHAPTER THREE

Two men camped in Utah's Provo Canyon in 2012. They filmed a black shape in the woods. It stood. They ran. Their video went viral.

People in Louisiana have reported a Bigfoot-like cryptid. Louisianans called it the Honey Island Swamp Monster. Others claimed to see Bigfoot. One or both of the creatures screeched. It sounded like a siren. In 2000, timber worker Earl Whitstine claimed he saw a hairy creature twice in a few days.

FAST FACT

People have reported several creatures like Bigfoot. In 1971, the Fouke Monster attacked a house in Arkansas. Reports of Florida's skunk ape go back to the 1940s. The skunk ape gets its name from the bad smell it gives off.

CHAPTER THREE

A Tennessee teen said he came face-to-face with a creature. The teen refused to share his name. He worried people would make fun of him. As he told a Library of Congress researcher: "It looks something like an old man and its face is, just looks like real tough hide. And it stands about eight or nine foot tall."

Bigfoot researcher Paul Freeman hiked in Washington state in 1994. One day he took film of footprints. He raised the camera. A dark shape crossed in front of him.

These kinds of stories convinced many Bigfooters. Other people wanted more evidence. But they chose to keep an **open mind**.

Scientists and other investigators, meanwhile, took a closer look.

FAST FACT

Bigfoot became a craze in the 1970s. Action heroes fought the creature on TV. Hairy cryptids scared moviegoers. Kids could play a Bigfoot board game.

CHAPTER FOUR

CASE FILES

A scientist gathers evidence. The evidence supports or fails to support the answer to a question. One question is, Does Bigfoot exist?

The evidence for the answer "yes" relies on eyewitnesses and footprints.

William Roe saw the creature as an eyewitness. Believers note he gave many details.

Skeptics ask tough questions. Why did Roe only come forward after the hunt in Harrison Hot Springs? Why did he never speak about the creature again?

CHAPTER FOUR

The Raymond Wallace case depended on footprints. Wallace died in 2002. His family admitted he faked the prints. A friend carved wooden feet. Wallace wore the feet and stomped around. “He didn’t mean to hurt anyone,” his son said. It turned out Wallace had played pranks his whole life.

Wallace steered Roger Patterson to Bluff Creek. Bigfooters believe Patterson appeared at the perfect time.

Skeptics say that thousands of people have searched for Bigfoot. Could Patterson really find the creature on the first try? An author named Greg Long investigated Patterson’s life. Patterson had been dishonest in the past. Friends said Patterson had hoped to make money on Bigfoot.

The Patterson-Gimlin film remains the strongest evidence of Bigfoot. Investigators like Jeff Meldrum think the film shows an unknown **primate**. “You can see muscle movements,” he told NPR.com. “You can see the shoulder blade slide under the skin.”

For now, Bigfooters and skeptics disagree.

FAST FACT

Bigfooters in Charlotte, North Carolina, created a hotline to report Bigfoot sightings. They called the hotline Bigfoot 911.

CHAPTER FIVE

MAKING IT UP

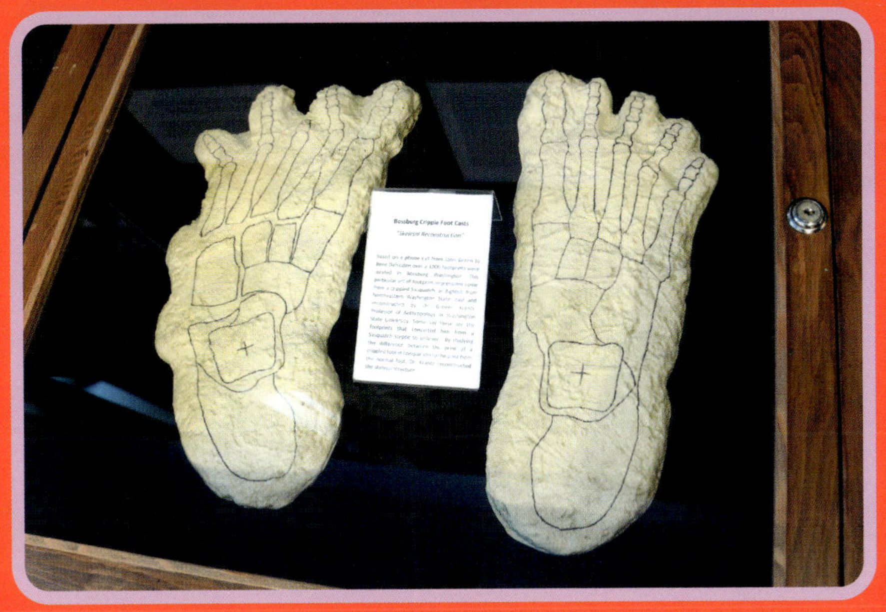

Raymond Wallace pulled off a Bigfoot **hoax**. Others have made up sightings and evidence, too.

Ivan Marx moved to Bossburg, Washington, in 1969. His goal: find Bigfoot. Marx found giant footprints. These tracks differed from others. The creature's right foot looked injured.

Bigfooters rushed to Bossburg. No one else found anything, except Marx. He kept stumbling onto footprints and other clues. One day Marx claimed to have filmed the creature. A Bigfooter named Peter Byrne paid Marx to put the film in a safe place.

CHAPTER FIVE

Byrne made his own investigation. His evidence showed the Marx film was phony. Then a local man admitted he made tracks in a nearby town. "I just wanted to show that anybody could fake them," the man said.

Rick Dyer called himself a Bigfoot hunter. He appeared online and on TV to discuss the creature.

Dyer claimed he shot a Sasquatch. In 2014, he charged people money to look at the 8-foot-tall (2.4 meter) body. But a company had made the Sasquatch out of latex, foam, and camel hair. Dyer had tried the same hoax six years earlier.

Bigfooters dislike hoaxes. A hoax makes people question all Bigfoot stories.

In the meantime, believers keep searching for evidence. As Professor Mark Collard noted to CBC.ca, "At this point, the only really compelling evidence would be something direct," like a skeleton or body.

FAST FACT

Peter Byrne was a well-known Bigfooter. Byrne found hair and skin after seeing a Sasquatch. Byrne sent the hair and skin to a laboratory. He hoped they would test what he had found. Forty years passed. The government released the results. The hair and skin came from a deer.

TIMELINE

6000 B.C.E.	Kwakwaka'wakw peoples already living in British Columbia
1920s	Members of the First Nations Sts'ailes community tell John W. Burns about the sasq'ets
1957	William Roe states he saw an ape-like creature two years earlier in British Columbia
1958	Raymond Wallace pulls a Bigfoot hoax using a pair of giant wooden feet
1967	Roger Patterson and Bob Gimlin make a film of what they claimed was Bigfoot
1971	Witnesses say the Bigfoot-like Fouke Monster attacked a house in Arkansas
2007	Rick Jacobs snaps a photo of a hairy bipedal creature in Pennsylvania
2014	Rick Dyer's fake Bigfoot body makes headlines
2019	The Federal Bureau of Investigation (FBI) reports that Peter Byrne's Sasquatch hair sample belonged to a deer

GLOSSARY

bipedal (BY-pee-el)
Using two legs to walk

cryptid (KRIP-ted)
An animal that no one can prove exists

evidence (EH-ve-dens)
Facts or information that indicates something is true

hoax (HOKS)
A fake or trick used to deceive others

icon (I-kon)
A person or thing important in a certain time or place

indigenous (in-DIH-je-nus)
The original inhabitants of a region

open mind (O-pen MIND)
A willingness to listen to or accept different ideas

primate (PRY-MAYT)
The group of animals that includes humans, apes, monkeys, and lemurs

skeptics (SKEP-tikz)
People who doubt or question an idea

FACT CHECK

1. A skeptic of Bigfoot would hold which belief?

A. Roger Patterson filmed a real Bigfoot
B. Bigfoot came from outer space
C. There is no evidence that Bigfoot exists
D. Bigfoot lives in Washington state, Pennsylvania, and other places

2. People describe which of these cryptids in the way others describe a Sasquatch?

A. The Honey Island Swamp Monster
B. The Jersey Devil
C. Chupacabra
D. The Loch Ness Monster

3. Sts'ailes storytellers originally described the sasq'ets (Sasquatch) in which way?

A. As large, colorful "birdmen"
B. As giant humans who wore their hair long and protected the land
C. As creatures made of ice
D. As tiny people who liked to play tricks

4. Which of these incidents was NOT a well-known Bigfoot hoax?

A. Rick Dyer displayed a fake Sasquatch body
B. Ivan Marx found giant footprints in Bossburg, Washington
C. Raymond Wallace used wooden "feet" to leave Bigfoot tracks
D. William Roe saw the Fouke Monster

Answers: C, A, B, D

FIND OUT MORE

IN PRINT

Beatty, Gayle, and Deborah Ray. *A Young Researcher's Guide to Bigfoot*. New York: Archway Publishing, 2017.

Halls, Kelly Milner. *Cryptid Creatures: A Field Guide to 50 Fascinating Beasts*. Seattle: Little Bigfoot Publishing, 2019.

Korté, Steve. *What Do We Know about Bigfoot?* New York: Penguin Workshop, 2022.

ON THE INTERNET

National Geographic. "Bigfoot's Big Foot." Via YouTube.com. Undated. Video.
www.youtube.com/watch?v=rvT17_Z_Tio

Oregon Public Broadcasting. *The Film That Made Bigfoot a Star*. Via YouTube.com. Uploaded April 12, 2019. Video.
www.youtube.com/watch?v=xVo6Vj0_Xbo

Public Broadcasting System. "Could Bigfoot REALLY Exist?" Pbs.org. Uploaded January 13, 2016. Video.
www.pbs.org/video/its-okay-be-smart-bigfoot

INDEX

About the Author

Kevin Cunningham has written over 120 books on history, medicine, careers, and climate change. He lives near Chicago, Illinois. He doesn't believe in Bigfoot, but he wanted to write a book to learn why other people do.